Intuitive Glow

A Poetry Collection

Jennifer Mormilo

BookLeaf Publishing
India | USA | UK

Made with ❤ on the BookLeaf Publishing Platform
www.bookleafpub.in
www.bookleafpub.com

Dedication

I dedicate this book to my mom, brother, and sister for always encouraging me to grow. I'm grateful for your love and strength.

Acknowledgement

For those who choose to read these verses, thank you. Your time and reflection have the power to make a difference. By exploring these ideas together, we create a space for connection, understanding, and growth in ways we may have never imagined.

Preface

Poetry illuminates the emotions we carry. The words in this book capture moments and thoughts that shape how we see ourselves and our world. We embrace the dichotomy of life through these contrasting themes of light, love, darkness and fear. However these words find you, I hope they bring warmth and meaning.

The Power of the Unknown

Power lies in the unknown.
Directionless until directed otherwise.
A path one paves based on love or hate—
the choice is yours.
It's like the cycling of water,
constantly flowing in and out, in and out.
An endless wave built by what's come
before it.
A steady sign of what's expected next.
A sense of unity or a sense of divide.
You decide.

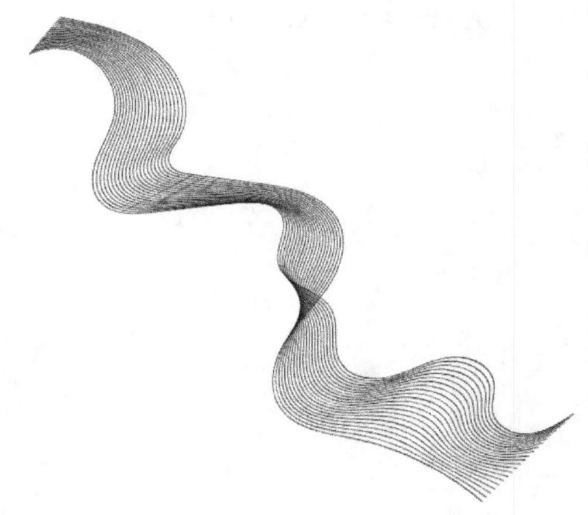

The Energy That Binds Us

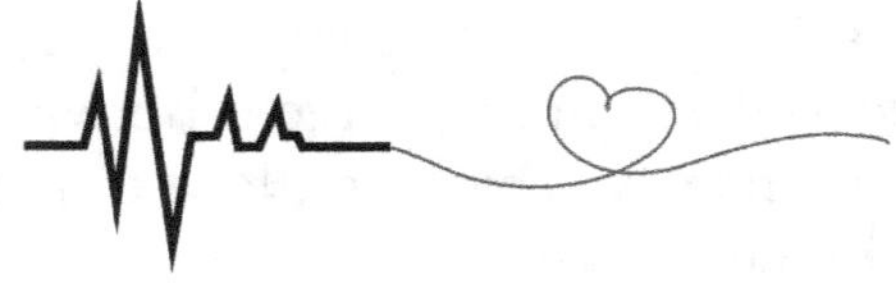

It is within the energy we do not see that
binds us for eternity.
Your heart beats; so does mine.
An ecstasy over time.
Movements turn to moments
remembered.
A steady resonance.

Beyond the Line

A line on a paper,
representative of boundaries not to be
crossed.
Guidance given to a society of those who
merely follow the rules.
But who's to say those rules should be
obeyed?
And more so, who defined the line?
It's likely someone you've never known
and someone you never will—
a directive given that's shaping your space
and time.
How cathartic does it feel to go beyond
the line?
Reaching new forms.
Setting new stakes.
Instead of being given your direction,
learn to read between them.
Learn to go beyond them.

Unseen Threads

A woman resides in Alaska.
A man plants his roots in Japan.
Opposite sides of the world,
yet tied by threads unseen.
The woman sits calmly,
music dancing through the air around
her.
She is at peace—
mind, body, and spirit in harmony.
The man is on the hunt,
seeking inspiration for his latest creation.
As she grounds herself,
merging with the almighty consciousness,
her vibration rises—
a ripple in the unseen tide.
Across the world,
the man feels a sudden jolt,
a pulse of energy he cannot name.
He stops at a garden,
standing before a quiet pond.
Looking down, he sees his reflection—

a full-body sensation,
knowing that all is well.
He returns home,
spirited, renewed.
His masterpiece—the pond.

A Vessel of Light

I create space around me—
a barrier of energy and light,
an unseen force that shields me
from the world's chaotic tide.
It is more than space—
it becomes who I am.
A force to be reckoned with,
divinely protected, universally connected.
But it stretches beyond the universe,
beyond the limits of thought.
I cannot name it,
but I can feel it—
a presence growing stronger each day.
Its essence deepens in every way,
as I turn inward, healing,
unearthing the child within—
standing tall, standing proud.
A subconscious vessel,
holding lifetimes of memory,
woven through space and time.
How sublime.

The Flicker of Fear

A light flickers.
The wind moves freely through the trees.
A voice is heard from afar, its face unseen.
Was it the wind rustling the leaves,
creating tricks in my mind,
making it hard to sleep?
I steer my mind toward a safer, warm
space,
envisioning a field of flowers,
frolicking with grace.
The battle continues.
Another creak causes my senses to rise.
My heart beats faster,
chills running down my spine.
Is this just a game, created through
imagination?
Or is the terror real, instincts guiding me
away from the situation?
I close my eyes,

anchor myself in warmth.
The mind is a master of illusions,
but fear—
fear is a willing student.

The Silence of Solitude

Sitting in silence,
I could hear a pin drop.
Heat spews down from the vent above my
head.
A faint sound of the TV hums
downstairs—
the only semblance of life surrounding
me.
I breathe in, a deep, hearty breath.
I breathe out, my lips emanating sighs of
relief.
The day is complete.
This moment of silence and peace—
a reverence to the constant movement
that has plagued my family's lives.
With each step taken,
each experience braved,
we move forward.

A Fleeting Connection

Walking down the street,
bundled against the cold,
the zipper of my jacket
clanking against my jeans.
A woman moves swiftly toward me—
a stranger I'll likely never see again.
Do I engage,
or keep my head down,
pretending that steadiness
matters more than connection?
In a split second,
my hand lifts—
a small wave,
a quiet smile.
Her eyes meet mine.
I'm met with a look of surprise.
For a moment,
confusion is her only reply.
Then, just as she passes,
the corners of her lips lift—
a silent acknowledgment,
a fleeting connection,
gone as quickly as it came.

Bridging the Seen and Unseen

I close my eyes,
about to journey toward a higher
vibration.
I open my chakras, one at a time,
envisioning cylindrical colors of light,
moving from the root of my being
to the crown above my head.
I bridge the gap between the physical and
the ethereal.
I set my intention, then ask for
permission.
Within moments, I begin to
see with my mind's eye,
hear with my inner voice,
know without clear reasoning.
I am connected to the divine—
the divine speaking through me
for the woman who sits beside me.
"Trust," the woman says.
"Trust the messages you receive."
I plant my feet further into the ground
below me.
I open my palms as my hands rest on my
thighs.
I have faith in this experience

and faith in that which I do not see.
A message is pieced together—
my first reading attempted.

The Weight of Uncertainty

Up and down like a rollercoaster,
flowing in and out like the waves of the
sea.
A flood of emotion takes hold of me.
Thoughts in my head
pull me in all directions.
Words are being said,
but their essence lacks resonance.
Spiraling like a staircase,
no clear ending in sight.
The nagging is so loud,
making this such a hard time.
I cry out for help.
Is this all just in my head?
I beg for some solace,
direction, and a plan.
Why do all things happen?
And why am I right here?
How come it's not clear?

Maybe it's all just an illusion—
one big video game of sorts.
What's the point? To look past fear?
To grab the world by its horns?
At times, life seems chaotic,
while other moments mute.
But maybe that's the premise,
for nothing to compute.
There is no right or wrong, I'm told,
and that's the part that gets me.
So long as my choices
be the ones that bring me peace.

The Echoes of Ancestry

Your features tell a story,
whispers of faraway souls
who walked the earth long before you.
Eyes, lips, nose—
each a fragment of another,
woven into your present form.
What unexplainable happenings
across space and time
led to this ideal moment—
a perfect creation—
for you to grace this planet?

The Power of Words

A blank slate,
tarnished by words.
A single line on a page,
now heavy with meaning.
In an instant,
an isolated object
intertwines with something new,
absorbing its essence—
never to be the same.

The Walls We Build

Incense burns from across the room.
I sit, questioning the things I do.
Trapped between compare and contrast—
a hell on earth, if it lasts.
Hands in shackles,
feet bound tight,
knees weak beneath the unanswered why.
How did I get here?
Who will set me free?
Who am I supposed to be?
Walls that have grown higher than
imagined—
a story of protection
turned into a story of isolation.
Try if you may, try if you might,
the only way in is to break the wall,
and it won't go down without a fight.

The Conditioning of the Mind

Mouths move on the screen before my
eyes.
Voices ramble,
spewing "facts" to the public—
believed unless told otherwise.
Truths entangled with lies,
a constant stream of content,
conditioning of sorts.
A brain on overdrive,
searching for a retort.
Reality fused with fantasy—
has far-reaching implications.
How does what we consume daily
shape our emotions,
our interactions?
Each experience molds us,
subconsciously feeding a beast
that takes over our minds.
Ingesting less poison,
while replacing it with love and
connection,
can lead our society to a more fruitful
union.

The Storm Before
the Light

Darkness falls upon me,
a feeling of dread hanging over.
Birds chirp beyond the walls,
but their songs cannot reach me.
Rain falls.
The earth drinks deeply,
parched for so long,
only to be drowned,
puddling in its own excess—
unable to withstand such sudden change.
A new day awaits,
the sun expected to rise,
ready to dry out the pain.

The Tug of Control

Hooked.
A reprogramming of the mind.
Daily mantras, daily meditations—
can there be too much of its kind?
Some days I feel aligned,
others, I slip—
hot and cold, on and off,
like plates shifting beneath my feet.
How do I stay grounded
when the world around me shifts?
I move through life like a game of chess,
always two, three steps ahead.
Are intentions ever pure?
Or is everyone just making sure their own
are fed?
There are two sides to every coin.
My aim is to see the good,
but when life throws storms,
sometimes I get lost in the flood.
So, I slow down, breathe,
find my center.
I let go of control,
leave karma to the healers.
Returning to my mantras
is returning to myself.
When peace lives within me,

then the world around me finds balance
as well.

The Weight of Fear

Are there fears that haunt you,
holding you captive,
keeping you from the life you seek?
Does what you know,
and who you've been,
align with who you are becoming?
If letting go feels like loss,
then how do you justify
the betrayal of self
when you choose instead to hold on?

The Art of Returning

I trace my hand,
like I'm back in the first grade,
when a simple connection of lines
could turn from the outline of my fingers
to the feathers on a bird's back.
When my outstretched thumb
could morph into a neck and head,
guiding the body that bore the weight of
wings.
At what point did I stop using
my simple imagination
to carry me beyond the ordinary?
We grow up taught to think,
to be a certain way,
but maybe that isn't the truth.
Aging is an unlearning—
a re-finding, a re-defining,
a return to what we knew all along.
Coming home.

The Rhythm of Connection

My energy rises to meet yours,
yours lowers to meet mine.
Two vibrations moving in sync,
drawn together by the opening of self—
a gateway to deeper connection.
Clarity emerges.
Beyond dimension, beyond form,
two worlds collide into one.
We are the same.
We must only open
our eyes,
our hearts,
to see it.

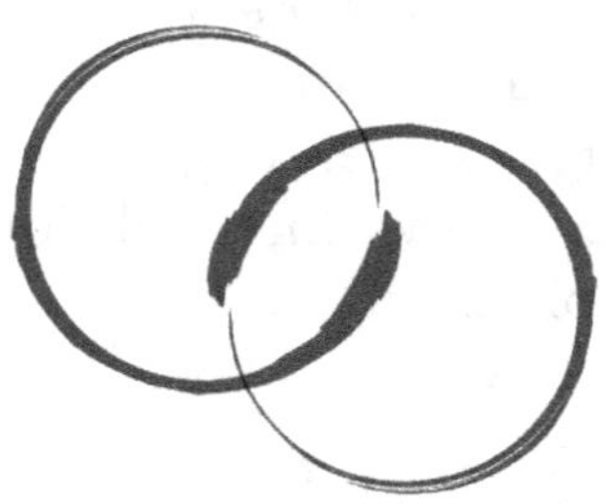

The Taste of Affection

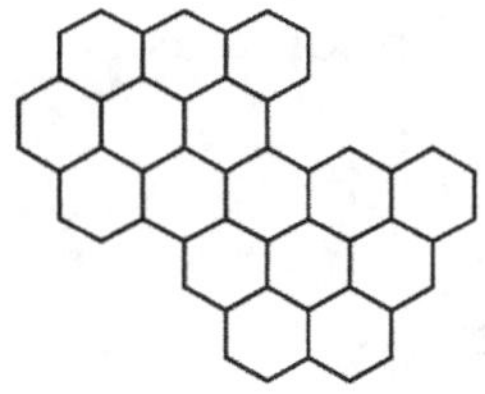

"Honey," he calls out.
Sticky to the touch.
Sweetness lingering on his tongue.
A nickname for her,
his favorite flavor.

The Simple Joys of
Life

Red lipstick—
smeared like jam on toast.
A raised glass,
a celebration of life.
Eyes open,
a new day begins.

The Weight of the
Game

This back and forth—
it's driving me crazy.
One minute we're good,
next, things get hazy.
They ask for a hand, then demand a
whole leg,
The pressure keeps building—
hell, do they want us to beg?
I search for hope in my heart,
ask God for forgiveness,
Place my faith in His hands,
and seek refuge from all of this.
I'm aligned with the process,
it seems this should be our path forward,
But why does life keep throwing obstacles,
making me question my choices?
I wish I could see the future,
know it'll all be okay.
The reality is, things are good now—
I'm just getting tired of the game.
It feels like I'm constantly being tested.
Is there ever an end?

Or, as bleak as it sounds,
does it stop only when I'm dead?

Maybe we chose this—
A life full of hills,
a journey of sorrow
mixed with elevated thrills.
If I've learned anything at all,
it's that I'm a real fighter—
Passionate, driven,
a crafty survivor.
No matter what comes,
we'll face it together—
My family and I,
unified forever.

The Illusion of Care

Toying with someone's emotions—
is that what it's called these days?
Sending texts, hanging on,
just enough to keep them at bay.
With chatter over time,
care starts to mingle with fraud.
And when you recognize the difference,
do you stop—or keep holding on?
At what point does it become harmful
to both you and the other?
As the behaviors persist,
does the truth become harder to
decipher?
Swept up in what now feels like a game,
the game morphing into your reality—
A reality built on intrinsic emotions,
mostly insecurities.
By acknowledging the fault,
do you acknowledge your role too?
And how do you move beyond awareness
to see real change through?
Does it stop once spoken,
said aloud for the world to hear?
Or does it stop only when the cycle
repeats,
happening to you, confirming your fears?
Whatever it takes—take more.

Take space.
Take time.
Know that cycles can be broken.
You just have to want it enough.

Breaking the Pattern

Back against the wall,
head propped up by a pillow—
Supportive, yet angled just enough
to keep a bit of discomfort in my body.
My attention shifts to my stomach—
another point of unease.
The food I ate tonight was healthy,
but overindulgence pushed me to the
edge,
a habitual pattern of shoving
a sugary dessert down my throat
afterward.
Why?
Because I'm conditioned.
Because sugar feeds me
in a way that maybe other things don't
right now.
But I know I need to break the pattern.
I know I need to hold myself
accountable—
long enough to say it's no longer in
control.
But is it?
Or does the action seem harmless enough
that the daily behavior justifies itself?
Ultimately, it doesn't.
And I know I need to be strong enough,

aware enough,
for just a moment each day
to make the next one easier.
But maybe it's not even a handful of days.
Maybe it only takes three or four.
Who knows?
What I do know is this—
I'm in the driver's seat.
I steer this ship.
And I get to decide
how dark the skies become
or how much light
I choose to see instead.

Fingers on the Keyboard

I bite my fingernail,
airPods in my ears—
Nothing but the silent buzzing
of sound frequencies passing through.
I place my fingers on the keyboard,
tap, tap, tap away at the keys.
The tapping turns to words,
words flow into sentences on the screen.
A rhythm woven together—
first in my mind, then before my eyes.
Thoughts once silenced
now alive.
Where do these thoughts come from?
How deep do they go?
Is the tunnel never-ending?
Is my mind a black hole?
One thought leads to another,
and the cycle persists.

But for a moment, I veer away,
shuffled in thoughts that don't connect.

Yet I return.
I pull myself back to the present,
let this moment take hold,
reel me in, taunt me like a sin.
But this process brings me joy,
even when it feels tricky—
trying to take what I'm feeling
and turn it into something beyond words
on a page.
Turned into messages born with the hope
that one day, they'll be shared with the
masses.
Even if it starts with just a few.
Because a few can spark change,
a few can leave a mark.
We just have to know it's true.

A Beat Beyond Time

Legs crossed, tanned socks hugging my
ankles,
toes wiggling beneath the surface.
My foot bounces up and down
to a melody only I can hear—
a tune playing in my head,
a current carrying me to faraway lands,
while my body remains grounded,
right here in my bed.
But I wonder—can you hear it?
Can anyone else hear this tune?
Hear my tune?
And maybe, just maybe,
someone, somewhere,
lounging in a completely different room,
in a completely different place,
is bouncing their opposite foot
to the very same beat.
That beat—now our beat.
A rhythm transcending.
A sound not just heard, but felt.
A beat that lingers,
a beat that lasts forever.

The Paradox of
Being

To be alive
is to be bold,
to be heard,
to be seen.
Yet, to be alive
is to be cautious,
to be silent,
to be invisible.
—

The weight of words,
the darkness before the dawn,
the chaos of the storm.
Yet—
The space between the lines,
the brilliance of daylight,
the stillness after the flood.
—

To be alive is to be everything and
nothing all at once.
To feel so deeply that nothing—
And everything—
is felt just the same.

It is the endless cycle of renewal and
decay,
a rebirth, a fading,
a rejoicing, a mourning,
a return to self, a loss of self.

Rewriting the Plan

She has a plan—
a plan to be and do all these things before
she turns 25.
— Skiiiiirt —
She's 26.
Now what?
—

She has a plan.
Version 2.
Things change.
Life moves like cars speeding down the
highway—
three lanes heading south,
two more merging from both sides.
— BAM —
Death. Loss. Healing.
She's 29,
facing new obstacles each day,
in a place she never expected.
But she still has a plan.
—

She pauses,
looks back at her life.
Leaves space to acknowledge
all that she's done,
all that's transpired.
— Beep beep —

She's 32.
Now realizing that life has its own plan.
And this whole time she's just been along
for the ride.
No matter what happens,
the plan is much grander than she knows.
All moments connecting,
woven seamlessly, effortlessly—
a plan created long before her birth,
a life remembered long after death.
So mote it be.

Fading Memories

Cherry.
One of the girls you and I both
remember—
a taste she wished stayed with you forever.
Blossom.
The trees that perfumed the gardens of
Brooklyn and Queens,
a spectacle worth an hour-and-a-half
journey to see.
Reminds me of another girl my sister
used to know,
posing me beneath a big willow.
Trying to capture a moment in time,
but like all things posted online,
these connections were fleeting.
Faded, then carried away by the wind.
Some memories cherished,
others best forgotten.
Experiences become lessons—
lessons we sometimes drown in.
Yet, they shape us,
Morphing us into the people we choose to
become.
With intentions of a more hopeful
tomorrow.
So let's give thanks to the moments that
led us here,

for the times that made us stand taller,
facing fear.
Through space and healing,
what once jolted us subsides.
Rebuilt like a craftsman's art,
golden lines glistening across the teacup,
Standing taller with pride.

Angel Numbers

111
Repeating numbers,
a new beginning each day.
222
Signals from the universe
telling me to stop worrying,
to trust in my path.
333
The ascended masters stand beside me,
guiding me to balance
my thoughts, emotions, and actions.
444
What I focus on becomes my reality,
as the angels surround me.
555
When I release what no longer serves me,
I make space for massive change.
666
I must remain connected to my soul
as I traverse this earthly plane.

777
Grounded in myself,
led by my spirit and my guides,
I am in perfect alignment,
ready to receive.
888
Earth-based abundance
flowing toward me on my path.
999
I keep moving forward,
making space for the new.
A positive mind,
an aligned body and soul—
manifestation at its peak.

www.ingramcontent.com/pod-product-compliance
Lightning Source LLC
LaVergne TN
LVHW021302200726
843509LV00012B/1752